The Weight of Feeling

by Rhett Ellis

The Weight of Feeling
© Copyright 2012 Rhett Ellis
Sparkling Bay Books

ISBN: (10 digit) 0-9670631-9-1
(13 digit) 9780967063195

Philosophy, Self-Help, Career, Business, Relationships

Acknowledgments

Thanks to MerriAnne Magdech for her editorial wisdom.

Thanks to Stephanie Lance for her professional analysis.

Thanks to Hope Bennett for her keen artistic insights.

Thanks to Dayton Cook for his excellent design of the book.

Contents

Introduction	5
Chapter 1	6
Chapter 2	8
Chapter 3	16
Chapter 4	20
Chapter 5	24
Chapter 6	26
Chapter 7	30
Chapter 8	34
Chapter 9	37
Chapter 10	40
Conclusion	43

Introduction

Every human decision and action is made on the weight of feeling. This is a truth so powerful that to master it is to master life itself. It is a truth so obvious and simple that it often escapes direct observation.

I discovered the feeling scale accidentally. I was a tobacco user who had "quit" a number of times only to return during times of prolonged stress or sadness. I started chewing tobacco at age seven, and having started so young, I got seriously hooked. I cannot imagine anyone more addicted or more controlled by an addiction. When I was a child, children could purchase tobacco, and I would use my allowance or the earnings from part time jobs to buy it at the gas station up the street from my family's house. I would hide it in a hole under the box springs of my bed where my mom would not find it, and I would sneak it to school in my book bag.

I am now in the longest stretch of my life without tobacco-- over ten years. I still think about it and even dream about it from time to time, but I remain tobacco free because of the way I quit. I will explain how I utilized the feeling scale to quit tobacco at the closing of this book.

The stories you are about to read are true. For privacy's sake, I have altered details in the stories, changed the names of characters, and created composite characters.

Chapter 1

We will start with a simple illustration of the scale at work.

Martin was forty two years old when Dr. McLeod gave him the news.

"You're going to need surgery," Dr. Mcleod said, "Without surgery, your condition will threaten your life. You could go today. You could go six months from now, but the odds of living more than two years in your condition are one to ten."

Martin drew a deep breath and began to take in what his doctor had said. Martin started weighing his feelings against one another on his feeling scale. On one side of the scale was Martin's trust of Dr. McLeod. On the other was Martin's distrust of authority, specifically his distrust of doctors.

Martin closed his eyes. Dr. McLeod had come highly recommended by two of Martin's friends. He considered the sincerity of Dr. McLeod's expressions and the concern and authority in Dr. McLeod's voice. Another opinion would be nice but time was a factor. Martin knew something was wrong with his heart. He could feel it as his eyes remained closed.

Martin pondered all factors available to him together. He also experienced the force of a subconscious factor—his need to believe. The weight of his trust increased against his distrust.

Martin's decision was simple, immediate, and overwhelmingly emotional. Martin released his breath and opened his eyes.

"I'll have surgery immediately," he said.

Illustration 1.1

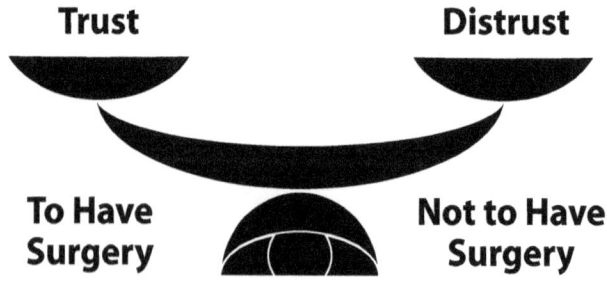

Jeanne married Dalton, her college boyfriend, two months after graduation. Within a year of the wedding, Jeanne knew that she and Dalton had little in common, but by then she was pregnant and she dismissed the thought whenever it came up.

Three years and two children later, Jeanne felt lonely most of the time. Dalton had never abused her, and they seldom fought, but that was because he seldom interacted with her on any level except for sex.

Jeanne began to ponder filing for divorce, but there were the children to consider. Jeanne asked Dalton to see a marriage counselor with her, but Dalton dismissed the idea with a laugh.

Around the same time, Jeanne met Kyle in an internet chat group. It began innocently, but Jeanne felt a connection to Kyle. That connection grew deeper with each conversation. When Jeanne was with Dalton, all she could think about was her conversations with Kyle.

Jeanne's feeling scale began to tilt back and forth on the question of divorcing Dalton to pursue a relationship with Kyle. In time Jeanne's feelings in favor of a divorce outweighed her feelings in favor of staying married to Dalton, and she left him for Kyle. Dalton assumed that Jeanne's decision to divorce him and begin a physical relationship with Kyle was all about sex. His assumption could not have been farther from the truth. Jeanne's sexual experiences with Kyle were not as intense as her sexual experiences with Dalton. It was all about Jeanne's heart feelings, and her feeling scale tilted accordingly.

Illustration 1.2

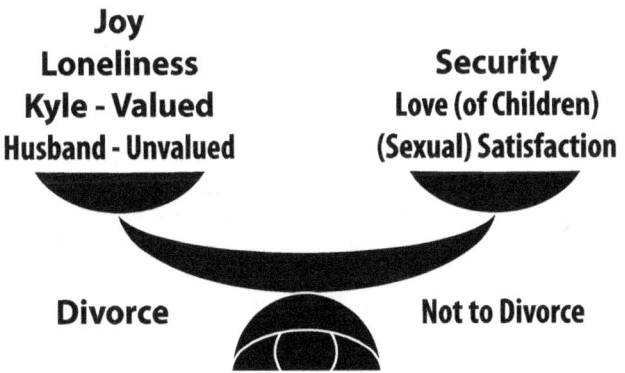

Chapter 2

Now lets take an inside look at the techniques of a small town business tycoon, a man who makes his living by buying and selling. His techniques are identical to those used at the highest and lowest levels of trade and negotiation.

When you meet Carl, you instantly like him. His large face, slightly round, slightly red, smiles all over, and his eyes twinkle. When he removes his cowboy hat, his white hair is neatly combed to the left. His belly hangs a little over his belt buckle and shakes with deep laughter. He's a clean shaven version of Santa Claus. When he reaches out to shake hands, his grip is firm, reassuring. When Carl sells you an item for thirty-percent more than its market value you feel like you got a bargain.

Carl learned many of the basic principles of the scale when he was a young man, and although he has not thought about them in those terms, they have served him well. After thirty one years in the furniture business, he knows surprisingly little about furniture. He doesn't have to know about furniture. He knows how furniture shoppers feel their way to a purchase, and he knows how to read and weight their feeling scales. His small town furniture business yields him an income equivalent to that of three average families, plus he makes an average family's income with his hobby of buying and selling used cars.

On a Thursday afternoon, during a lull in his furniture business, Carl reclines in his office, loosens his tie, and clicks on an internet site with classified ads. He knows just the kind of car he is searching for, one old enough not to be covered in the value guides. This guarantees the value of the car will be widely open to opinion and discussion. He finds just the one, a ten year old, mid-size, two-door family model of Japanese make. The paint looks good, high mileage, but not high enough to completely devalue the car. A car like this could be the best purchase someone ever makes, or the worst, and there is no way of knowing beforehand.

Carl calls the owner and asks a specific set of questions. He listens to the answers, but more importantly, he listens to the inflections in the owner's voice. He notes the things that make her nervous or excited. When her tone of voice is tight, and her words sound like they are sticking in her throat, he knows she's nervous, unsure of her statements. When she sounds relaxed, he knows she is confident. Carl hears what he hopes to hear. As the six year owner of a ten year old car, she is certain that the car has been well maintained. As a non-professional, she is not sure about the asking price, which Carl knows is low.

The most revealing of answers is to Carl's question, "Why are you selling the car?"

"I'm a school teacher, just got on at a new school, and bought a new car. I didn't think they were giving me a fair offer on this car as a trade so I'm selling it myself."

Carl appraises her emotional state. He knows that with the down payment for the new car, the increase in insurance, and the payments coming soon, she feels she needs to sell soon. He agrees to come have a look at the car after work, and they agree to a time.

If Carl is interested and unless another buyer is more interested, the seller's ultimate decision will be: do not sell the car to Carl or accept Carl's highest offer. Even before he sees the car, Carl has his highest offer in mind and a strategy to weight her emotions to accept it. The negotiation process will seem arbitrary and random to her. She will have no idea that she is dancing to Carl's tune from the first step to the last. Carl's singular purpose will be to get her to accept his price. That one purpose will guide every word he says.

Carl arrives, takes a glance at the car, and strikes up a friendly conversation. "Where're ya from? Oh, I know some folks up that way (Carl knows people from everywhere)... Do you know old so-and-so? No? What about so-and-so? Yes? He played baseball with my son, almost like a son to me, used to spend time at my house."

Carl is weighting her feeling scale with familiarity, connectedness, friendliness, and warmth, all on the side of accepting his highest offer.

Carl works his way around the car, checks the tires, the headlights, under the hood, and comments on various strong and weak points but more importantly he takes the conversation in a personal direction, asking open ended questions to get the owner to open up emotionally. "How do you like teaching? Don't know how teachers do it in this day and age, so different from when I grew up. My hat's off to them. Do you have family in these parts? I know it's a way off, but you would be welcome to visit my church sometime, it's real friendly. What a beautiful sunset, would you look at that?"

Carl adds two more feelings to the side of accepting his highest offer—

insecurity about the value of the car and personal connectedness to the seller.

Carl loads his conversation with words meant to inspire positive feelings, comfort and hope. He watches the seller's body language as she relaxes.

He says that he likes the car and explains that if he buys, he will not have to ask for time to arrange financing. He has cash at home. He watches her eyes, the involuntary twitch of her lips. At this point, he has a solid idea of the outcome of this deal. Now it is just a matter of completing the process.

He takes the car for a test drive, and when he returns, his face is slightly gloomy. He thanks the owner, and says he will need to go home and talk it over with his wife. This is always a risky maneuver as this could leave the owner open to another purchaser, but that is part of the game.

By walking away, Carl deepens the owner's feelings of insecurity about the value of the car. Is the asking price too high? Will she get even less than the dealership offered her for a trade? Will she get any money for it at all? This introduces the emotion of impatience into the equation.

The next afternoon after school, Carl calls the owner and says that after talking it over with his wife, he can offer her the equivalent of half her asking price. She protests that the car is worth much more than that. In a tone warm and a little sorrowful Carl points out things he noticed that needed repair or replacement. The tires are thoroughly worn. The breaks are not tight. A tail light cover is cracked. There are several stained places in the upholstery. He would have to put money in the car to get it up to standard. He apologizes for taking up her time… and hesitates.

She reflexively asks Carl for three quarters of her original asking price, meeting Carl half way. Carl says he will have to talk that over with his wife and asks for time. An hour later, Carl calls and raises his offer but stops just short of half way to her new asking price. As expected, she drops her price half way to Carl's price, and Carl accepts, explaining that he feels sure his wife will be okay with it.

The next afternoon when Carl and one of his employees drive over to pick up the car, the seller is all smiles, feeling like she did a good job of negotiating, when the fact is, Carl got the car for less than half of what he will sell it. When she signs the title over to Carl, and Carl places the cash in her hand, she breathes a deep sigh of relief and involuntarily gives the kind and grandfatherly Carl a hug.

Illustration 2.1

The next morning, Carl has the employee spray some engine cleaner under the hood, rub a coat of wax on the body and polish it, and steam clean the interior. By noon, it is ready for the "for sale" sign.

Carl sells the car using the same techniques in reverse. He offers it for sell at a price much higher than he expects to receive so that after negotiation, the purchaser thinks Carl really got pushed around on the deal. Instead of pointing out the car's flaws to potential buyers, he points out every good thing about it. Most importantly, he waits. He refuses to be intimidated by the flow of time. Time is Carl's best tool.

Carl's furniture store purchases furniture from a variety of sources and in a variety of ways-- importers from third world production companies, close outs and returns from big city stores, slightly damaged items from high-end factories, auctions, a few used items, and a tiny number of new items from respectable wholesalers. The key consideration when purchasing is the lifestyle of the small town, middle class customers to whom he sells. They are not the residents of New York City high rise condominiums using furniture to make statements about their status. They get together to watch college football on autumn Saturdays. They invite guests over after church on Sundays to drink coffee and eat pie. They like to sink down in the cushions, recline, and take naps after work. They value functionality, simplicity of style, and comfort. Name brands mean almost nothing to them.

On a Tuesday morning, a recently retired couple comes into his shop. Carl greets them with a smile like he had just run into his long lost best friend.

"Can I help you find something, or are you just looking around?"

"Just looking," the woman says.

"Well, take your time," Carl says, "and if I can help you just holler."

Carl walks slowly over to his elevated check-out counter and shuffles through some papers. As the couple strolls and discusses the appearance of various pieces, Carl eavesdrops. He discerns that they are in no hurry to make a purchase. Most of their furniture is in good shape, and their motivation for being here is mainly to pass the time. They wouldn't mind making their den a little more hospitable for visits with the grandkids, but if they buy anything it will be because they have found a deal just too good to pass up.

Carl looks the man over, "Excuse me sir, about twenty years ago, did you play softball in the summer league?"

"Yes, I did."

"I thought I recognized your face. Who'd you play for?"

"East Side Auto Parts, one year, Wesleyan Church, the next."

Carl smiles, "Wesleyan beat my team for league championship, were you on that team?"

"Yes, I was, did you play?"

"Nah, I have trouble with my back, and doc says I can't, but I coached Carl's Furniture."

Carl casually continues, finding mutual acquaintances, bringing the woman into the conversation, reminiscing, and joking about old age. He talks about anything and everything but furniture. He creates an atmosphere, a mood, a feeling of understanding.

He doesn't attempt to sell them anything, but when he senses the conversation has almost run its course, he says, "Just to let you know, I've got a wrap-around, detachable sofa/love seat combination coming in on Thursday. I bought it at auction as damaged at the factory, a small tear on the back side of the sofa, but if you place it against a wall, it's not even visible, just an amazing deal, really. If you want first dibs on it, I'll call you as soon as it arrives.

"Okay," the couple smiles, and Carl takes their phone number. First dibs on an amazing deal… who wouldn't want such a privilege, especially a couple in need of diversions and with plenty of time on their hands?

The decision to return to the store seems like a small one, but of all the decisions people make on a regular basis, the choice between boredom and stimulation is the one that makes the world go around. It is pre-weighted on the side of stimulation.

Carl's goal is to get them to buy the couch at his target price or higher. The couple's goal is either to hold onto their savings or to accept what they perceive to be an excellent deal.

On Thursday morning, Carl calls, and they drive to his store. Carl knows this will have to be a soft sell, so soft that the couple will think they are leading the way through the thought process. When they arrive, Carl is on the phone. He has a pen behind his ear and is shuffling through some papers. He motions them toward the rear of the store and points to the piece.

They walk over and begin to inspect it as he continues to talk. Its rich brown suede is soft and appealing to the eye. They sit on it, recline in it, and wait for Carl. This is part of his plan.

Out of the corner of his eye, Carl watches them smile and nod in agreement that this really is a nice set. Now it is time to start. He picks up a catalogue and walks over at a slow, even pace.

Carl chuckles, "can I wrap it up and send it to you?"

The couple laughs.

"Just kidding with you," Carl says, "but let me tell you about this set. It was made in the same factory that makes the name brand sets that look just like it, same everything." Carl shows them a picture in the catalogue. The couple is impressed, but their eyes grow large at the staggering price.

"Well," Carl continues, "this is not the name brand, same exact design, but nowhere near that price, and this one is discounted on top of it. Have you seen the tear on the back?"

"Yes," the woman says, "really not that bad."

"Not bad at all," Carl says, "and I've got an upholstery guy who can make it almost disappear. Back it up to a wall and it won't matter at all."

Now Carl begins to plant ideas, "I own a set almost just like this one.

My granddaughters are just crazy about it. The littlest one curls up and sleeps on it while the older one watches TV."

This registers with the woman. Carl knows that she is imagining her own grandchildren on this sofa.

"I like to kick back on it and watch football," Carl says. The truth is, Carl is not a football fan, but he sees the man take the bait. The man smiles and Carl knows he is imagining himself watching his favorite team.

Carl continues planting dreams and feelings, some of them only indirectly connected to the set, all of them good. He gently helps them convince themselves that this furniture is the gate to utopia.

"Okay," the woman says, "drawing in a deep breath, how much is it?"

Carl quotes a price that brings a frown to their faces, but before they say a word, he recovers with a big relaxed smile and a chuckle, "That's just the sticker price, I'm sure we can do better than that. Also includes delivery and installation."

The couple relaxes a little, and Carl invites them into his office. He knows he must not place them in a "yes or no" situation.

"I don't want you to answer me today," he says, "I want you to think this through. A piece of furniture like this is the center of a family's home life, a once in a lifetime purchase."

To the couple this seems a kindly gesture to relieve them of pressure, but it is just the opposite. Carl is buying time to build even more pressure.

Carl goes through some papers, makes a couple of calculations, and offers them a reduced price.

"Now, I'm not saying this is my final price, but I won't be able to come down much from here. Just think about it, sleep on it, and if you like, we can talk later."

On Friday morning, Carl calls the couple. The husband answers, and Carl says, "I've got another couple who is looking for a piece like the one I showed to you. Now, I promise I won't offer them a better price than what I offered you, and I won't show it to them at all if you want me to hold it. What do you think?"

The answer is not of great importance. If the man says Carl may show it to the other couple, this creates competition, a fight for the deal of a lifetime in their mind. If the man asks Carl not to show it, the sell is done.

"Let me ask my wife," the man says, and this is a positive sign for Carl. This implies that the man is willing to buy it and has left most if not all of the decision to the woman. From here through the rest of the process, Carl will do everything he can to weight the woman's feelings. The woman says Carl may show the set to the other couple, but this is not troubling news to Carl.

On Saturday afternoon, Carl calls the couple. The woman answers, and he says, "The other couple that looked at the furniture passed on it at the price I showed you. They made me an offer I will accept, but I told them I promised not to sell it at a lower price until I had given you and your husband the chance to decide. I can hold it until Monday morning if you would like to take another day to decide."

They talk it over and, no surprise to Carl, call on Monday morning. They agree to buy at the reduced purchase price.

Illustration 2.2

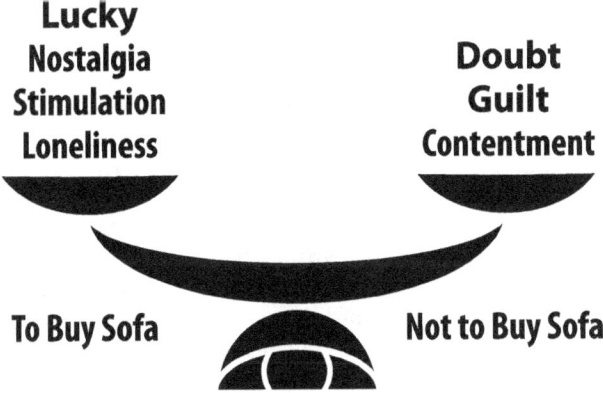

There was no other couple.

Chapter 3

Every year, women and men lose enormous amounts of their income to the "attraction industry." They buy gym memberships, hairstyles, clothing, etc. yet they often ignore the central and key issues of emotion. Attraction is a simple matter of tilting the feeling scale of whoever we wish to attract. Once we know the correct weights and place them on their scale, attraction comes easily and naturally.

Maria is no beauty queen. She has pretty eyes and a good complexion, but her legs are disproportionally short. Her nose is crooked. Her hair is kinky and she is flat chested. The best word to describe her appearance is "cute," not "pretty" or "gorgeous." On a scale of one to ten, Maria is a six and a half, but on her college campus, she manages to attract more boys than many eights or nines.

At a campus social, she laughs and smiles all night. She is constantly amused with life, and she plays her way through it, even when she is working. Where other young women are serious and burdened, she is unconcerned and carefree. When a student organization on her campus invited her to march in protest of environmental abuse on a Saturday morning, she said she would rather sleep in protest of environmental abuse. When another organization asked her to "adopt a child" for the monthly cost of a soft drink, she said she would make a terrible mother because she liked soft drinks.

She is not dependable, something of a user, but to be near her is to feel your long lost, careless inner child coming back to play. She is fun, charismatic, radiant. When relating to men, she gives them only a hint of herself, a laugh at their jokes, a punch on their arms, and then she vanishes.

Not in spite of but because of her attitude, she easily gets what other girls find difficult to acquire. On dates, the other girls talk to the young men about long term goals, work, family, and other such mundane, dreadful subjects. Maria talks about music, movies, and her favorite cartoons. Without trying, she inadvertently creates an atmosphere of fun, and the boys compete to be chosen.

Using the feeling scale to compare Maria and the ordinary girl quickly reveals why men break in the direction of girls like Maria.

Illustration 3.1

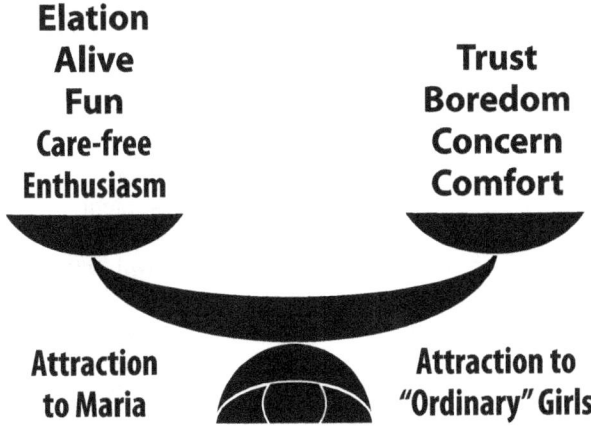

Beauty occupies a prominent place on men's internal scale of attraction and no woman hoping to attract or maintain the attention of a man should take it lightly, but there are intangible qualities that weigh as much, and for most men, much more. Generally speaking, men love the feeling of pursuing a woman. They do not like to be pursued. They prefer freedom to captivity, fun to commitment. The elusive, the unattainable, the intangible joy of life, this is what attracts men.

Some of the same may be said of women, but as a rule, when weighing attraction women are more complex.

When he was in his middle fifties, George's wife of thirty-one years passed, and after a year and a half of mourning, he decided to re-enter the world of dating.

George tried an internet dating site but was unimpressed with the quality of women who responded positively to his ad. He complained to a friend of his, an art instructor at a junior college, who was also middle aged and in the dating game, and his friend offered to help with the ad.

The first thing his friend changed was George's description of himself. Despite plenty of available space on the site, his original posting was short, blunt, unimaginative, and altogether uninteresting.

It read: widower, store manager, high school graduate, enjoys golf and boating, seeks companionship.

His friend changed it to read: After thirty one happy years of marriage and a long battle with cancer, my beautiful wife departed this world to fly into the sunset and stars upon which we often gazed. That was over a year and a half ago. Though the pain of losing her lingers, I thought I heard her whisper to me in the evening wind that she would be happy if I moved on now and found companionship.

It has been awhile, and I'm not sure how it is done these days, but here goes: I am the general manager of a local branch of a successful store chain. I did not attend college, but I have learned plenty in the school of hard knocks and have risen through the ranks of three companies. For exercise and relaxation, I enjoy playing golf with my friends twice a week. It is a hobby, not an obsession. My other hobby, however, is an obsession. I am an avid boater. The rolling of the waves, the feeling of the wind in my hair, the sound of seagulls-- all of it adds up to a feeling of joy. It is on the water that I find my truest and deepest self.

My ideal companion must also enjoy the water. She must be physically fit, mature, and ready to pursue all of life's joys, prepared for life's sorrows. She must be flexible, easy going, and eager to make new friends. If things work, I would like to introduce her to my children, relatives, and long-time friends who are of supreme importance to me, and I would look forward to meeting her loved ones.

The new ad weighted the feeling scale in George's favor:

George initially posted one photo, a posed portrait in which he is standing against a wall and staring into the camera with blank eyes and a contrived smile. This photo was a negative weight on the scale:

His friend did two things to improve his image. First, he dug through George's old photos for pictures that told stories. One was of George presenting a plaque for employee of the year to a young man at the store. George was wearing a suit and tie in the photo, and the young man was wearing a store uniform. The picture conveyed George's status as a leader of men, a success, the kind of man who presents awards to those beneath him in rank.

Second, he asked George to meet him with his boat at the docks for a photo shoot and to be sure and wear his skipper hat. His friend snapped a number of photos of George looking natural, thoughtful, and at peace. Then his friend asked a couple of young bikini clad girls on the beach for some help with a photo shoot in exchange for beer. They agreed. He asked them to wrestle George's skipper hat away from him, and caught it all on camera. There were smiles and laughter and playfulness. Perfect strangers, these girls, but looking at the photos you would think they were old pals of George's.

The artist had everything he needed. He uploaded the photos to George's page, opened it for viewing, and the response was overwhelming. The new photos weighted the scale in George's favor:

Local women responded. Women in other states responded. Older women and younger women, professional women and women who had never worked responded. George had become the most eligible man in his age bracket, and for three months he had as many dates as he wanted including the one with the lady who would become his companion. She owned her own boat.

Illustration 3.2

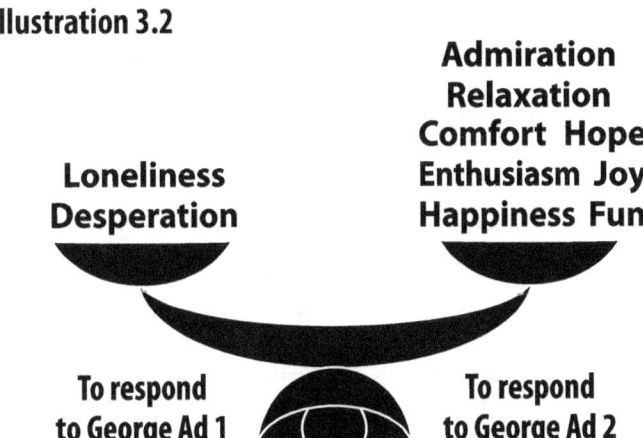

The feelings we project are the feelings others accept. If we project attractiveness, we will be attractive. Looks, fitness, grooming, and even financial well-being all play their role in the game of attraction, but the condition of the inner-being is what wins in the long run, and the inner being can be strengthened as well as better communicated.

Chapter 4

The burden of subconscious weights affects the effectiveness of a person's feeling scale. Weights of the subconscious resist most attempts at removal, especially direct attempts. They can skew a person's judgment so severely that their every decision may seem exaggerated or irrational. A subconscious weight may make its presence known in a range of ways, from self-destructive habits to magnificent accomplishments and often both simultaneously.

Peter's father was a perfectionist. If his father asked him to wash the car, Peter would do his best, but his father would always give it another going-over. Peter was clumsy and never excelled at the sports he attempted to play, and though his father told him he was proud, Peter could see in his eyes and hear in his inflections that his father really was not proud of him. Peter's mother offered little solace. An intensely religious woman and an obsessive germ-a-phobe, she made Peter feel dirty all the time. For the blue collar area in which they lived, Peter's upwardly mobile family made more money than most, and the small amount of status this bestowed on him guaranteed little sympathy from friends and extended family.

From childhood, Peter's scale was weighted with deep insecurity, feelings of inferiority so deep and intense they colored everything Peter did.

When Peter graduated college, he got a middle management job with a small gas station chain. Within a couple of months, his bosses recognized his intense work ethic. Whereas his peers worked ten hour days, Peter worked fourteen to sixteen hour days, and hour for hour, he did twice as much work.

As the chain grew and opportunities for promotion became available, Peter received them first. He was awarded plaques for his achievements in the company, including employee of the year during his first year.

If you were selling Peter a car, and if you had mastered reading feeling scales, like Carl the furniture salesman, you would only need to insinuate that the car in question was a symbol of true manhood. Peter would find such a car nearly irresistible.

One Saturday night Peter went out to a bar and began to drink heavily, a practice that was becoming a habit. When he drank, Peter was able to smile. When a stranger at the bar, an older man, invited him to shoot some pool he agreed to a game. Peter missed what should have been an easy shot, and the stranger laughed. Peter chuckled along with him, walked around the table, and for a moment stood beside the stranger as he lined up his shot. When the stranger took aim, directing all his attention to the table, Peter lifted his cue and brought it down with demonic force to the back of the stranger's head. He continued to savagely kick and beat the stranger until two bouncers arrived and pulled him off of him.

The beating was caught on camera, and Peter could have gone to jail for it, but his company helped him locate and hire the best lawyers. The stranger agreed to a settlement, and the matter was dropped.

Peter's sex life was limited to prostitutes, a habit he acquired in college, but at one point he began to date an attractive young woman who marketed snack products to his company. He quickly became attached to her to a degree that frightened her. When she stopped seeing him, he left desperate messages on her answering machines, messages with an undercurrent of anger that intensified her fear. He knew that he was driving her away, but he could not stop himself from dialing her number.

When it was obvious to him that she was never going to return his calls, Peter dusted off his old hunting shotgun, a gift from his father on his twelfth birthday. He had never been able to kill anything with the gun, both because when it came to animals his heart was tender and because he was a poor shot. He loaded it, placed the butt of the gun on the floor, the tip of the barrel in his mouth, reached down, and pressed the trigger.

All but one person at work agreed they could not have seen this one coming. "Anyone but Peter," they all said. He was positive all the time, so full of energy, such a hard worker. The one person who was not shocked was the head of the company. He had read Peter's feeling scale the day he hired him and had been making use of his pre-existing weights from day one.

Peter had attempted to balance his feeling scale, or better still achieve self-respect through effectiveness at work and an attempt at a relationship…

Illustration 4.1

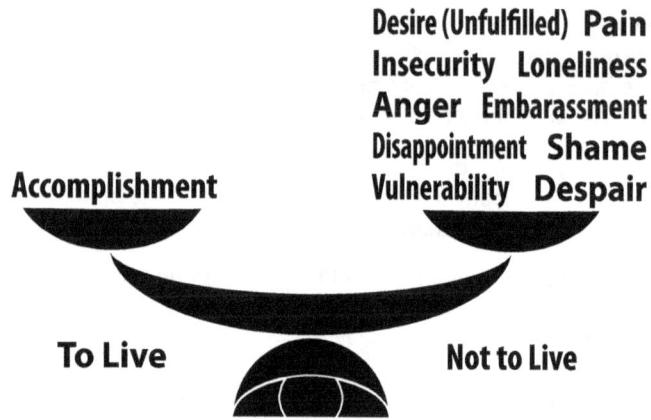

But failing to understand his own core feelings, he could not. By attempting to change his internal state through external means, he was actually working against his best chance of happiness. Introspection, meditation, and therapy would have been his best first steps toward unburdening his scale.

Brittney's senior year of high school was full of glory and smiles. She was elected homecoming queen by a large margin, and waving at the cheering crowd, rode on the hood of a Cadillac across the football field. The team quarterback, who was also the class valedictorian and her boyfriend, was her prom date, and they were elected queen and king. She was captain of the cheerleading squad and a talented softball player.

Brittney didn't take her grades too seriously because she didn't think she had to. She had no professional aspirations except perhaps to work as a cosmetologist someday. Until she made up her mind, she would wait tables and see her boyfriend on weekends.

A month after he started college, her boyfriend broke up with Brittney. Three months later she started dating a classmate who had become a construction worker upon graduation. He got her pregnant. They got married, and settled into his trailer on the outskirts of town.

Brittney is forty years old now, and divorced. She still waits tables at the local diner. If you stopped in her town on a Friday night during the fall and attended the football game you would see her sitting in the bleachers, wearing her school colors. Both her children have graduated now, but she continues to attend the games. She bears the weight of faded glory, the weight of a good past.

Brittney wears entirely too much makeup, short, tight pants, and glittery midriff tops designed for women half her age. If you were selling Brittney a used car or a piece of furniture, you would only need to bring up that night she was paraded across the football field or the night she held onto the quarterback's arm as she received her costume crown.

The "good" women of her town talk about how loose Brittney is. It seems all a man has to do is adore the little beauty that remains to her, and Brittney is ready to sleep with him.

Brittney does not realize that even a glorious past is the past, and the past is dead. A good past is a heavier dead weight than a bad past. Brittney could easily right her scale with an intense focus on the present and an emotional divorce from the past.

Illustration 4.2

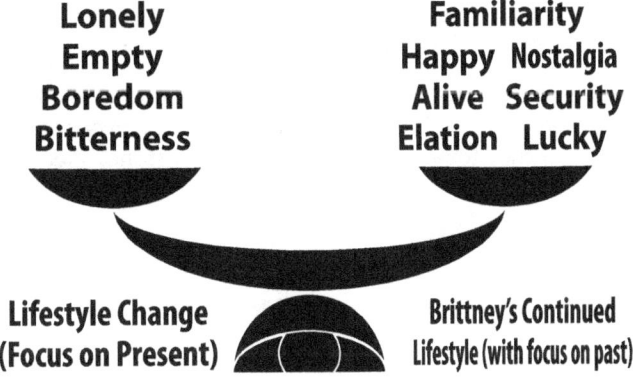

Taking time to examine the weights on our own scales is the first step toward righting our scales. Understanding the continuous weights on the scales of others is the key to understanding others.

Chapter 5

Professor Rene Girard wrote extensively on the role of mimetic feelings, especially mimetic desire, and although some of his assertions may be a bit extreme, I believe the subject is worth consideration.

We are prone to have some feelings simply because others have them. These are mimetic feelings.

A man from a primitive village takes a swim in a river, holds his breath, dives, and comes up with a stone. It's a smooth stone, colored a nice shade of blue. He likes the stone and carries it back to the village. He begins to braid twine for a necklace with a sling for carrying the rock. Another man from the village notices the work he is putting into the necklace, notices the stone, and offers some meat in trade for it. The man who found the stone refuses.

The man who made the offer tells another man about the stone, and the third man becomes obsessed with it. As he speaks his obsession to other residents of the village, desire for the stone spreads, even to those who have not seen it. In a short time, magical powers are attributed to the stone and, hoping to find good luck, a villager who feels his luck is bad murders the finder of the stone.

This is an example of mimetic desire-- desire for something mostly because others desire it. There are many stones in the river, some more beautiful than the stones we idolize, but once a stone is idolized by some, it tends to be idolized by all.

Illustration 5.1

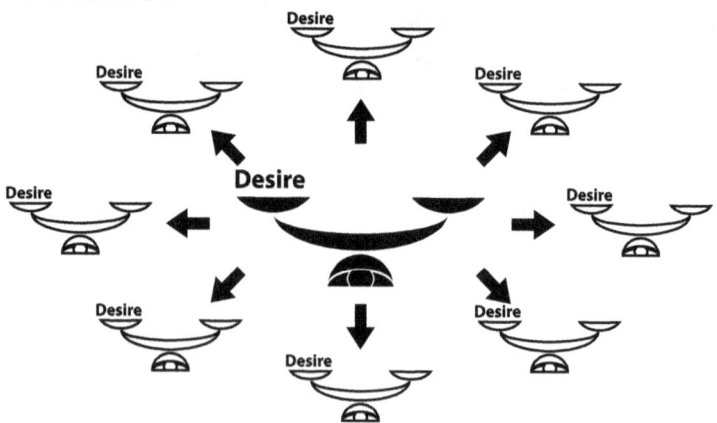

There are celebrities who are not particularly talented or attractive, but once they are established as celebrities, they remain celebrities simply because they are celebrities.

When I was in my early teens, a friend and I went hiking in a wilderness area with dense weeds and bushes. An armadillo darted from some weeds and brushed against my leg. For a moment, I thought it might have been a snake, and I yelled. Even after I recognized it was just an armadillo, I continued to yell. My friend yelled with me. When we caught our breath, I asked him why he yelled, and he answered, "I yelled because you yelled." His fear was mimetic.

I spent a few years teaching, and in each class, one or two strong personalities would establish the personality of the class as a whole. Their attitudes would spread verbally and silently from student to student. To deal with those strong personalities was to deal with the class as a whole, and each class had a personality of its own. Some classes were a joy to teach, others, misery, depending on the dominant personalities.

James was an average guy in a large high school. He was somewhere near the middle of his class in social standing until through a combination of unusual chances he began to date one of the most popular girls in school. Suddenly, girls who would not have given him a second glance were writing him notes, requesting his friendship on social networking websites, sitting beside him at lunch. Male classmates who had not previously noticed his existence began to invite him to their parties.

When the popular girl broke things off with him, his standing slipped. However, since the popular girl had established him as desirable, a girl only slightly less popular made an immediate play for him.

Mimetic feelings may have little or nothing to do with reality. One of the heaviest weights of feeling occurs when reality-based feelings and mimetic feelings combine.

Chapter 6

Moderation, discipline, and will-power are celebrated as virtues. People with the ability to follow their best desires can accomplish almost anything. They can quit bad habits. They can maintain many aspects of their health including their weight. They can strengthen the quality of their relationships. They can bring great good to the world, and hopefully bring no harm.

The factors that contribute to the ability to control ourselves are physiological, psychological, conditional, and environmental with overlap between all four factors. All factors create weights on the feeling scale.

With an unprecedented abundance of food, many, and in some countries most, of the residents are overweight. Most who diet fail to stay at their optimal weight, and within a few months of achieving their goals are heavier than before they dieted with a higher fat percentage.

This is not a diet book, and I am not offering a miracle plan for weight control. What the feeling scale offers to the health conscious is a tool to build their motivation on the side of their goals and preferred lifestyle. Be sure to consult a physician before starting any weight loss plan.

Fran was thirty pounds overweight and mildly depressed. She dreamed of what her life would be like if she were skinny. She imagined the men who would ask her out on dates and the possibility of meeting her ideal mate. She imagined days spent at the beach in un-bashful bathing suits. She attributed her every life-difficulty to her weight and imagined utopia on the other side of a good diet. She got into the latest fad weight loss program, reached her goal over a five month period, relaxed, relapsed, and gained all the weight back plus a few pounds more. Her story is typical and easy to picture on the feeling scale.

Illustration 6.1

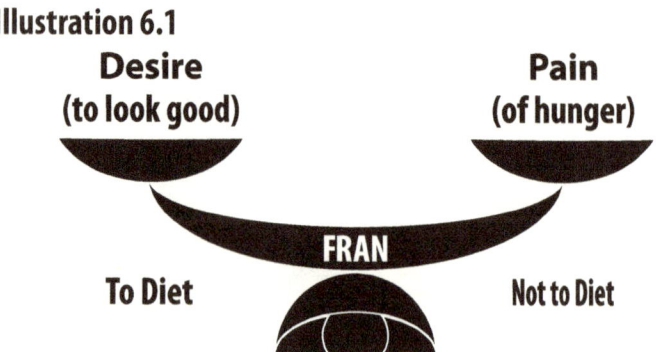

Because of Fran's narrow focus, the weight of her pain of hunger outweighed her desire to be thin, and in time this resulted in physical weight gain. Fortunately Fran eventually found a better way. We will return to her story at the end of the chapter.

William was jolly, easy going, and a hundred and twenty pounds overweight. He often made jokes about his size. He said he had tried dieting but that his glandular issues kept him on the heavy side. William enjoyed life, had plenty of friends, and was resigned to being unable to do anything about his health.

After experiencing weakness and fatigue, William visited his doctor. His doctor ran some tests and three days later called William back to his office. William's doctor explained that William was in the early stages of type-two diabetes. William had two options: maintain his current lifestyle and face an array of health problems, eventually develop type one diabetes, and take insulin shots to stay alive; or start and maintain a healthy diet, reduce his body fat percentage, exercise, and live well.

His doctor's speech was impacting. Among other things, it so happened that William hated needles. He vividly pictured himself in the poorest of health, and fear took over. William got healthy and stayed healthy-- walked two miles every day, ate healthy foods in reasonable quantities, dropped junk food from his diet altogether. The effect of the warning was essentially the same as that of Bill's warning in chapter one-- do or die.

Illustration 6.2

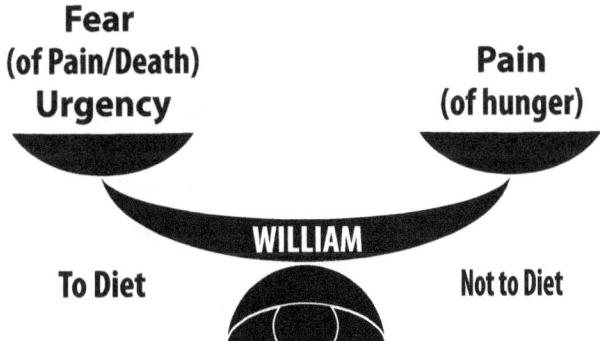

Ironically, people who would like to get in better shape but do not have a life threatening disease to motivate them may be at a disadvantage. Their best motivation may have to be abstract and intangible. Participants in extreme sports such as iron man competitions or mountain climbing often give spiritual explanations for what motivates them—a desire to be strong in their inner being. Properly weighting the feeling scale to simply maintain one's health is a significant challenge that may involve multiple life-issues, moderation, and differing motivations at different times.

After a divorce in her early forties, Fran decided to give getting in shape another try. By this time, there was a plethora of information available, and Fran chose yoga as her starting place. The meditation and relaxation techniques of yoga gave her a deeper and stronger foundation for overall health. She practiced guided imagery, especially imagining herself in her best shape. She kept a photo diary of herself at various levels of fitness. She got involved with and made friends in exercise groups, ran 5Ks and 10Ks, and kayaked beautiful rivers. She refused to date men who were not into exercise and when she did date, she preferred exercise dates. She took healthy-cooking classes and eventually taught a community education course on low fat cooking. The simple feeling of breathing deeply during exercise, oxygen rushing through her body, feeling alive—this became a major part of her motivation.

Fran struggled with the same existential questions with which most people struggle during mid-life. She chose life, and made quality-of-life her focus. She weighed the quality of life she enjoyed against the pain of hunger, which lessened over time, and the tired and occasionally strained muscles, and quality of life weighed more. Multiple interconnected feelings on the side of good health were the key.

Illustration 6.3

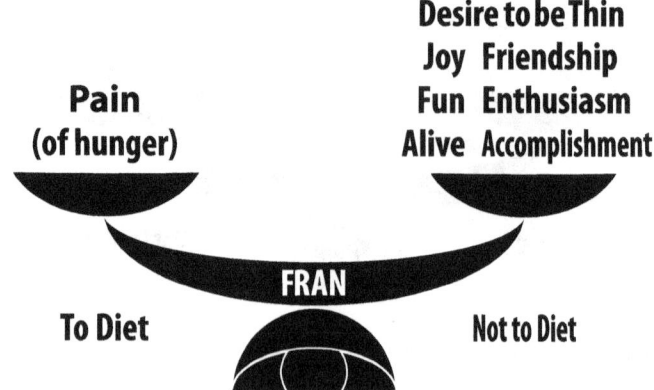

One useful key to attaining self-control through the feeling scale is to define negatives as positives. If discipline is required, a pain is involved-- hunger, boredom, fatigue, stress, cravings. When those negative feelings exist, give them names that give rise to positive feelings. When you feel hunger, call it "the-weight-loss-feeling" and value that feeling as a good friend. For someone whose health demands weight loss, hunger can be a good friend.

By association, weight is moved from one side of the scale to the other. If you experience boredom during some tedious but necessary task, call it "the-success-feeling." Connect as much of any necessary negative feeling to the positive side of your feeling scale as you can, and the scale will be weighted more to the positive side. Although the focus of this chapter is weight loss, the principle is valid for many pursuits where self-control is required.

Illustration 6.4

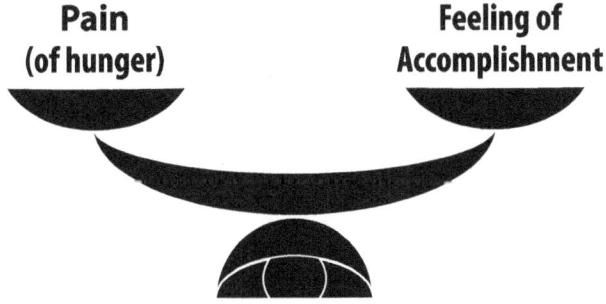

Chapter 7

The feeling scale can be used in connection with our subconscious as a powerful tool to get past delusions, accept truth, and enjoy a life grounded in reality.

Conscious, subconscious, psyche, heart, soul, spirit, mind, and other words have been used with a great amount of overlap to describe various functions of our inner being. Describing and defining what-is-what on the inside is no easy task, but one thing is certain-- a part or parts of our inner-being hides things from other parts. Delusion is a strong and constant self-defense mechanism. Delusions protect us from truths that we fear would destroy our minds if we believed them.

A person able to eliminate their delusions possesses an enormous power. Delusions, as comfortable as they may seem, hold us back. They prevent us from being who we really are and achieving the things we most want to achieve.

Martin was clumsy and weak. He was bullied in school, and immediately afterward applied for a job with the police force, passed the written test, and enrolled in the police academy. From the moment he put on his cadet's uniform, he began to have pictures made. Over the course of his career, he would have many pictures taken of himself in uniform. He had many of them enlarged, framed, and hung in his home and office. He gave them to the girls he dated.

When Martin pulled a driver over for speeding, he walked and talked in a manner reminiscent of a cowboy, often giving the drivers a good laugh as they drove away. When in uniform, he spoke in a voice that to him seemed demanding and forceful but was betrayed by the fact that his voice was naturally high pitched and whiney. This too gave a good laugh to many, both his fellow officers and the general public. All but a few were careful not to let him hear it.

One of those few laughed in his face during a routine traffic stop. Martin ordered him out of the car, and arrested him for disorderly conduct.

Martin began to have a recurring dream of a skinny tree bending and turning in the wind, back and forth, until it snapped. He would wake up immediately after the dream, sweating, and with his heart racing. The dream worried him so much he eventually made an appointment with the police force counselor to discuss it.

Illustration 7.1

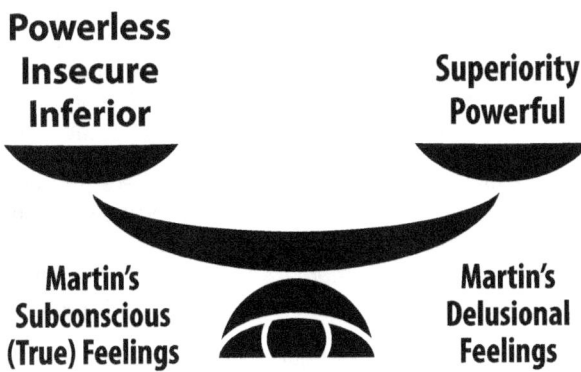

The counselor recognized the meaning of the dream immediately, but she had to find a gentle way to get Martin to see it for himself. A direct confrontation would have been too much for Martin's fragile self-image. He would have told his fellow officers that the counselor was incompetent and deserved to be fired.

Over a series of four visits, the counselor asked Martin questions about his childhood, about his choice to join the police force, and about his work. She worked hard to gain his trust, to make him feel respected, not judged. She worried she was getting nowhere until during his fifth visit Martin mentioned an insecurity. For the next two visits, she carefully worked her way around the edges of the insecurity, being careful not to confront it directly.

At the beginning of his eighth visit, Martin opened up completely without any prompting and broke down crying. This was the beginning of a healing process that ultimately led to Martin resigning from the police force, which he had never really liked anyway. When he gained enough security in his unique personhood, as opposed merely to his manhood, he felt comfortable pursuing the occupation he had dreamed of entering since boyhood-- carpentry. His uncle hired him to work for his construction company, and because Martin enjoyed his work, he became very good at it.

The counselor merely helped Martin realize what he knew all along. All the information was available in his subconscious, and his subconscious was screaming it to his conscious through his dreams.

The subconscious is by no means infallible. The subconscious does not know all the truths of the universe, but it is especially knowing and truthful where human relationships are concerned. The human body speaks a language louder than words. Professional gamblers can read the smallest of twitches, but there is a means of reading a person's inner-being that goes beyond logic or external observation. The "gut feeling" is a natural sympathetic response that connects people to each other subconsciously.

Mothers often know when their children are lying because they are so attuned to their children's honest facial expressions, relaxed body language, and truthful tones of voice that the moment (or even the moment before) their child lies, it registers in the mother's subconscious. The mothers feel what they themselves would feel if they were about to tell a lie.

Polygraph machines generally are effective because the subconscious betrays the conscious attempt to lie. This is a survival instinct built into our highly social species that keeps us from easily betraying each other. Some individuals are so sensitive to others' subconscious states that they are more effective than polygraph machines. They read people so well that they know things they cannot possibly know by any rational means. I have spent time with a few people of this high level of intuitive knowledge, and the experience can be quite eerie. It is no wonder that throughout history, their abilities have been attributed to the supernatural.

The intuitively gifted are in touch with the deepest levels of their own subconscious. Like mirrors reflecting a person's image back to them, they reflect back a person's deepest self-knowledge.

There are means by which a person may come into better and deeper contact and harmony with their own subconscious. Despite being called "lie detectors" polygraph machines do not detect lies. Polygraphs merely detect changes in a person's emotional state as it is expressed physically. When someone lies, their blood pressure and pulse rates increase, their breathing becomes irregular, and the electrical conductivity of their skin and muscles changes as a nervous response. Put simply, the entire body feels it when we lie to others or to ourselves.

The first step toward learning our subconscious truths and eliminating delusion is to learn our own bodies' feelings when telling truths or lies. Try this: Find a quiet place. Sit comfortably, close your eyes, and hold an object at arm's length. The object should be heavy enough to thoroughly engage your arm muscles but not so heavy as to be immediately tiring-- for an average size person, a cup of water should do.

Speak a truth (for instance, state "my name is" and say your name) and see if the object feels heavier. Speak a lie (state a name different from your own) and see if the cup feels heavier. For most people, the cup will feel heavier as they lie. Make a list of truths and lies, close your eyes, and learn the feelings associated with speaking them. From concentrating on your arm, move to your stomach and throat, which for most people are emotional centers. Note well the feelings in your throat and stomach as you tell truths or lies.

As you learn your own feelings, practice without holding an object. Just feel. Just know. When you are certain you know the feelings of truths and lies in yourself, you may begin to probe your subconscious. At first, this may be an excruciatingly painful process.

A person may ask a question such as "does my spouse really love me," and if the answer is "no," there may be enormous pain in the short term. However, in the long term a person can only gain by learning the truth. Perhaps the marriage can be saved by a deepening of communication and sharing of life experiences, but if the marriage cannot be saved, it is better to know this sooner than later.

Illustration 7.2

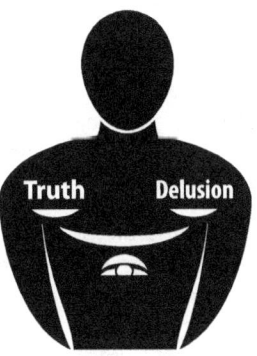

Again, I want to emphasize that the subconscious is not infallible, and sometimes our gut feelings are completely wrong. A woman felt that a certain man was a criminal of the worst sort because he always seemed nervous. The man himself could not explain why his feelings ran to extremes, why he often felt fearful for no reason at all. He later learned that he suffered a life threatening hormonal disorder that guaranteed him little ability to control his emotions. He was not a criminal, just a nervous person by nature.

Though the subconscious is not infallible, I am convinced that more often than not, what we feel at our core is likely to be true.

Chapter 8

A person's or place's "aura" is its intangible presence. The instantaneous feelings that are generated in us by someone or someplace come from their aura. I do not mean to imply that we have literal "energy fields" but there is a noticeable emotional atmosphere attached to many kinds of persons or things.

I believe the determining factor in every election since the first televised presidential debates has been the personality, indeed the "aura" of the winning candidate. Videos of debates and other appearances of the candidates are available online, and you may check my theory by feeling your way through each of them. The important thing is not to consider the content of the platforms but what the personality of each candidate makes you feel, their aura of words and appearance.

In 1960, after eight years as vice president during the mostly prosperous Eisenhower administration, Richard Nixon should have handily beaten John F. Kennedy for the presidency. In debates and interviews, Nixon came across as knowledgeable and intensely focused, but internally glum and stilted. Kennedy came across as warm and hopeful. Kennedy won.

In 1964, compared to Lyndon Johnson, Barry Goldwater seemed harsh and inflexible. Johnson, though not the most charismatic of candidates, was the master of the folksy, common touch communication style. Johnson affected a warm, hopeful aura, and he won.

By 1968, Nixon had learned the art of personal charm. I believe he carefully studied it as an art because when you compare his appearance in 1968 with his appearance in 1960, it is like watching a different person. In 1968, Nixon affected a regal aura. He looked and acted like a president and this carried him past Hubert Humphrey, who despite being a great orator, did not project a presidential personality equal to Nixon.

In 1972, against George McGovern, Nixon repeated his performance with even more charm and won.

In 1976, Jimmy Carter's personality was a breath of fresh air in American politics. His slogans were repeated often, and impersonators did his relaxed southern accent with a smile. Ford came across as stiff, worn, and half-hearted in his pursuit of the office. Carter won.

By 1980, economic upheaval and international crises had worn Carter thin. Carter looked like he had aged twenty years in four. Ronald Reagan, a Hollywood actor, was the perfect picture of charm, warmth, and confidence. Reagan won.

Illustration 8.1

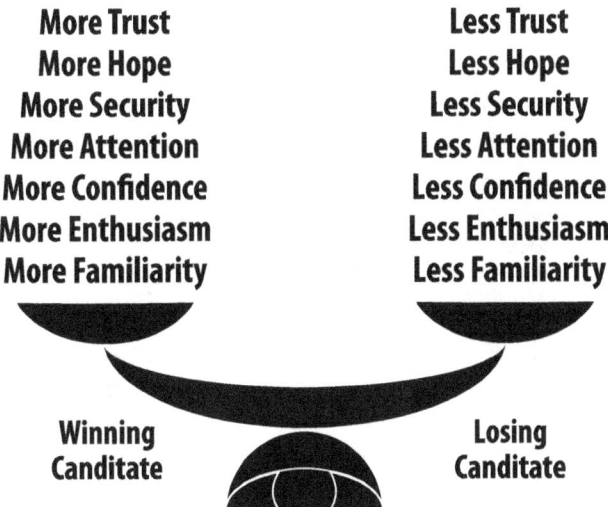

What is the "aura"? What makes it work? Consider the experiments conducted by John Bargh, Mark Chen, and Lara Burrows at New York University (published in the journal of Personality and Social Psychology, 1996, Vol. 71, no. 2, 230-244.) They gave tests loaded with sets of particular kinds of words then watched the reactions of the students. They gave a test with words related to rudeness such as bold, brazen, bother, and obnoxious. They gave another test with words related to politeness such as cordially, courteous, appreciate, and graciously.

The students then took their tests to a "grader" who, while talking to someone else, would postpone grading it. Those who took the tests filled with rudeness words would almost invariably react to the grader with rudeness. Those who took the tests filled with politeness words would almost invariably show extraordinary levels of politeness and patience. The students had been subconsciously primed by the tests, and their behavior reflected it.

Each of us has an aura of words and appearance. The words we choose, the clothes we wear, the way we carry ourselves-- these load the subconscious of those with whom we come in contact. Military officers wear more elaborate uniforms than enlisted soldiers. They demand to be addressed with specific words of respect. The uniform and culture of the officer is designed to create an aura.

Not only do we have personal auras, businesses have auras, houses have auras, cities and even countries have auras, and they weigh heavily on the feeling scale and have major consequences. Restaurants that succeed in creating an enjoyable ambiance, for instance, often succeed even if the food is inferior.

The auras we create and project have an immense impact on how we are treated and whether we succeed in our pursuits. This is not to say that we should be pretentious, indeed we should not because people would pick up on that immediately. The most powerful aura of all comes from deep genuineness.

The feeling scales of those with whom we come in contact will be weighted on one side or the other by a multitude of small details, a cloud of emotional stimuli. To seek out persons and places with good aura is an excellent way to build our own. The best way to create a good aura is to cultivate and project what is best in us.

Chapter 9

Weighting your feeling scale on the side of what you most desire may be easy or difficult, depending on your goals. I am going to suggest ten techniques that may help. Some goals may be so difficult that you must utilize most or all the techniques or create your own techniques.

1. Use photos and videos. Many inexpensive electronic options are available for documenting your past and your progress. Images have a powerful impact on the human psyche. Using photos and videos to record the happiness, growth, and rewards of moving in the direction you most deeply desire serves as reinforcement and a prominent weight on your feeling scale. For instance, if you have started a diet and exercise program, photos of your progress may serve as constant motivators.

2. Practice journaling. A written record of your life, whether kept private or made public, written from your feelings, with feeling and aimed at your feelings, may serve to weight your feelings on the side of what you most desire. You can use your journal to make a written contract with yourself. After starting a business, for instance, a journal can help you stay motivated by tracking your success and the feelings that came with it.

3. Visualize. Visualizing doing something is a major step toward doing it. A friend of mine held the record for the longest hitting streak on his college baseball team. His mental preparation was as important to him as his physical preparation. Before each game, he would rest, close his eyes, and picture himself hitting the ball. Not only would he visualize the process he would bring to mind the sound of the bat striking the ball, the feel of the bat in his hands, and the roar of the crowd. He mentally crafted a vision and stepped into it in reality.

4. Meditate. The practice of resting the body and focusing seems to work for its practitioners. Any practice that relieves stress, causes relaxation, and brings balance to one's emotions is a great starting point for weighting the feeling scale as preferred. Visualization can be done in connection with a meditation practice.

5. Use "mantras." By mantra I mean repeating a phrase, either out loud or to yourself, until you have internalized the words. A recording device may help in the use of mantras. Repetition is the key to learning. We learned our alphabet by repeating it out loud. We learned numbers by counting out loud. We can tilt our feeling scale by speaking to the side we wish to weight.

6. Try hypnosis. Hypnotism varies from person to person in degrees of success. If you choose hypnosis as a means to weight your feeling scale, be sure to use a licensed professional with proper training. Take someone you trust along to witness the process.

7. Create a positive environment. Our physical environment has an enormous impact on our emotions. If we surround ourselves with images that encourage us and reinforce our goals, we will be more likely to achieve them. If our environment is warm and soothing, we will feel better. A bright, clean environment inspires feelings of hope. Shape your environment to support your goals.

8. Surround yourself with encouraging friends. Human nature is so mimetic that we become the company we keep. Our feelings will inevitably resemble the feelings of those with whom we associate. Even one negative or positive friendship can have a drastic effect on the way we feel. A few years ago, one of my closest friends chose to discontinue associating with me. At first, I was sad about the loss and hurt, but in a short time I noticed that my overall mood changed. My outlook on life improved. I felt better about the future and my relationships. I am by nature a fairly cheerful person, but I had been subconsciously sponging his attitudes, his feelings. Getting some distance from negativity caused improvement.

I am not encouraging snobbery or isolating people with pain in their lives, indeed not, but we must take care of our own emotional health and well-being before we can help anyone else. I refuse to be bogged down in friendships or other relationships that poison my feelings. Instead, I search for and build upon the kind of friendships that encourage and uplift. I am then able to share my own feelings of hope with those in need of hope. Beyond basic friendships, encouraging friendship groups can make a positive difference in anyone's life. Support groups, whether formal or not, are of great value.

10. Condition away phobias. Do the thing you are afraid to do. I have a natural fear of heights. When I took a job that required me to climb to high places, I forced myself to do it. Over time, the fear of heights subsided. By confronting our fears, forcing ourselves to do things that frighten us, we outgrow them. As fear becomes less of a weight on our feeling scale, our scale will weigh more important emotions more accurately. Although an activity like mountain climbing and an activity like returning to school may seem completely different and disconnected, one may serve to build a positive attitude for the other. The can-do attitude learned in one activity

can be transferred to another, and one activity can serve as a symbol for another. By doing the things we fear, we build internal strength.

If these techniques are not enough, do not hesitate to seek professional counseling and/or medical care. Many of our emotional struggles are biochemical in nature and cannot be helped without proper medical treatment. Often a combination of medical care and positive practices such as the ones listed here can be used in conjunction with each other to build up our internal state. The motions of our life begin in our emotional core. We will do what we feel. Time spent strengthening and positively building up our feelings is time well invested.

Chapter 10

In this chapter, you will find a blank depiction of the feeling scale. You have my permission to make copies of it for personal use. You will also find an alphabetical list of words that describe feelings. I culled the list from many lists. I included one word that I did not find on any list: oughtness, the feeling that something was intended, predestined, or meant to be. I encountered this word in a source I can no longer recall. Of the lists I reviewed, some only included a few basic feelings, some include hundreds of words. You may wish to make your own list.

There are myriad combinations and possibilities for loading a person's feeling scale. You can use the illustration of the scale and this or other lists to visualize internal states. You may use the scale for self-understanding, self-adjustment, or in connection with others' feeling scales. Just place the words where they fit on the scale and where you would like them to be.

Accomplishment	Admiration
Alive	Amusement
Anger	Anticipation
Apprehension	Awe
Bitterness	Boredom
Bravery	Calmness
Comfort	Concern
Confusion	Contempt
Contentment	Confidence
Courage	Care-free
Disappointment	Disgust
Desire	Despair
Desperation	Detachment
Distrust	Doubt
Ecstasy	Elation
Embarrassment	Empty
Enthusiasm	Envy
Familiarity	Fear
Free	Friendship
Frustration	Fun
Gratitude	Grief
Guilt	Hatred
Happiness	Homesick

Honor	Hope
Humility	Indifference
Innocence	Insecurity
Interest	Inferiority
Joy	Jealousy
Kindness	Loneliness
Love	Lucky
Lust	Need
Needed	Nervousness
Nostalgia	Openness
Oughtness	Pain
Panic	Patience
Peace	Phobia
Pity	Pride
Rage	Relaxation
Remorse	Sadness
Satisfied	Security
Serenity	Shame
Shyness	Sorrow
Shock	Stress
Strong	Suffering
Surprise	Suspense
Suspicion	Sympathy
Terror	Tired
Trust	Urgency
Vulnerability	Wonder
Worry	

As you make decisions about weighting feeling scales, your goal must be to get beyond the drawings and lists. One masters the use of the feeling scale when one relates emotion to emotion, feeling to feeling directly without even having to visualize or make lists. Mastery is the ultimate goal. Years of practice may be necessary to attain mastery so be patient with yourself.

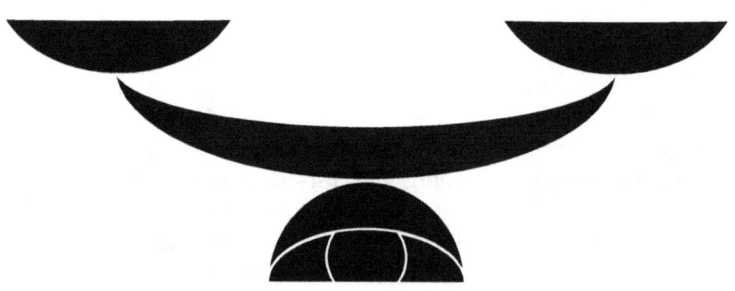

Conclusion

You now understand the basics of the feeling scale. As I mentioned in the introduction to this book, I accidentally discovered the feeling scale when I successfully quit using tobacco.

Because I did not want her to be disgusted, I was hiding my habit from the girl I was dating at that time. She accidentally discovered my tobacco pack and confronted me about it. I asked myself over and over why I was so weak, why I lacked the will power to quit tobacco once and for all. I got online to research the subject and happened upon photos of victims of cancer from tobacco use. I saw jaws cut off, grape size tumors under facial skin, tongues removed, and many other pictures of pain and sadness. This became a weight on the side of quitting tobacco.

The addictive desire for tobacco was heavy, a driving force in my feelings. The weight of the photos was heavy too. I stared at them, allowed myself to feel them, and submerged my emotions in the tragedy of their pain and loss. What little will power I possessed plus the weight of my feelings from the photos plus my desire to have an honest relationship with my girlfriend finally outweighed the desire for tobacco.

I quit, and for the first two weeks, the feelings on both sides of the scale were so close to evenly balanced against each other that I thought I would go insane. The tobacco craving was constant and strong, but the greater weight was on the side of quitting. For the next six weeks, the craving gradually weakened, and the scale tilted more to the side of tobacco free. After a year, the desire, though still intact, was so light against the joy of remaining free that tobacco was no longer an intense struggle, just a mild temptation to avoid.

Seven years later, I was working at a restaurant where the manager was a tobacco user. I told him about how I quit. He laughed, removed his pack, and waved it under my nose.

"Sure you don't want some?" He flashed a wicked grin.

The smell was instantly intoxicating. I knew what I had to do, and I did it quickly. I visualized the photos. I recalled the feelings that tipped the scale in favor of quitting.

"No, thank you," I said.

To control yourself, understand the scale of your feelings and weight it on the side of what you truly want to do.

Around the time I was outlining the thoughts that would become the basis of this book, I applied for and received a position of leadership in a small non-profit organization that had been in a state of decline for about two years. The number of members was dropping rapidly, and participation in service, activities, and events was waning. My goal was to reverse these trends.

From the beginning, I implemented the principals of the feeling scale. I made it my primary purpose to create a good mood throughout the organization. I filled my speeches with the most humorous and inspiring stories I could find. When I addressed life's hard side, I did so with words of hope and comfort. I went out of my way to have meaningful conversations with all attendees. Before attending meetings, I would eat well to get in a good mood, which I hoped would influence everyone else's mood.

I did not propose changes to the organizational structure, and I introduced only one new program— an ongoing, informal coffee/tea get-together with no other purpose than to enjoy socializing. I concentrated my efforts on changing the organization's emotional atmosphere and did not swerve in this effort.

Although the rolls were open for new memberships at all times, there was an ongoing quarterly event to welcome new comers into the organization— the customary point at which to join. Near the end of my first quarter in the position, the event was held. It was the best attended event of its kind in the living memory of the organization and resulted in a ten percent increase in membership.

Membership in the organization grew for three consecutive quarters thereafter, representing a twenty-five percent increase in membership in my first year. A significant number of inactive members returned to active service. Participation in all regular events and activities increased by no less than double digit percentages, and the organization returned to high levels of effectiveness in fulfilling its purposes. The principals of the feeling scale worked!

To lead others, understand the scale of their feelings and weight it on the side of what you want them to do.

In closing, I would caution you to be prepared for significant, intense change as you practice and utilize the feeling scale.

Also by Rhett Ellis:

The Wisdom of Shepherds is a novel so full of suspense, mystery, romance, adventure, and good humor that you will find it nearly impossible to wrench your attention away from its pages.

The Greatest White Trash Love Story Ever Told is an engaging tale of loss and redemption, pain and humor, loneliness and love. Readers report having found hope and encouragement in this strange, surprising, fun story.

www.ingramcontent.com/pod-product-compliance
Lightning Source LLC
Chambersburg PA
CBHW031438040426
42444CB00006B/866